THE CANDLEMAS LECTURE
on CHRISTIAN LITERATURE
1947

BOSTON COLLEGE CANDLEMAS LECTURES
ON CHRISTIAN LITERATURE

THE HERESY OF COURTLY LOVE

Alexander J. Denomy, C. S. B., Ph. D.
Pontifical Institute of Mediaeval Studies

WITH AN INTRODUCTION BY

William Lane Keleher, S. J.

President of Boston College

New York
The Declan X. McMullen Company, Inc.

IMPRIMI POTEST
    E. J. McCorkell, C.S.B.
        Superior General

NIHIL OBSTAT
    Edward G. Murray, D.D.
        Censor librorum

IMPRIMATUR
        Richard J. Cushing, D.D.
    ✠ *Archbishop of Boston*

November 4, 1947

THE HERESY OF
COURTLY LOVE

INTRODUCTION

INTRODUCTION

WITH the lecture that appears in the following pages, Boston College inaugurated a series which we hope will outlive any of us and will be as distinguished for its contributions to scholarship as for its length of days. We have called the series "The Candlemas Lectures on Christian Literature." In general, they will have for their subject some aspect of that extraordinarily broad and rich field of letters which has been inspired by and presided over by the spirit of Christianity. It goes without saying that no single lecture—indeed no series of lectures, however long—could present comprehensively that field or even any considerable part of it, and in this series we hope only to throw open a door here and there down a long corridor of more than twenty centuries. We cherish particularly the hope that some young students will be stimulated by the series to enter by one of these doors and to give their talents to appraising and making available the wealth that lies behind them.

The word "wealth" is chosen advisedly. Shall we begin with the Scriptures? The Old Testament, as one of the Fathers of the Church has splendidly said, is pregnant with Christ; the New Testament is the record, now greatly simple, now breath-takingly lyrical, of what the same Christ said and did. Shall we begin at a later date, when, more truly than at any other time, there was one fold and one shepherd, when "Jerusalem blossomed in the noon-tide bells"? Shall we, rather, begin nearer to our own day, and discover what Christian men, crying out of the depths of complex modern living, have imperishably said in verse or prose? One feels very like the traditional miser, letting gold coins drip through his fingers, as one meditates the names: Alcuin, Anselm, Augustine; Bernard, Bonaventure, Bossuet; Catherine, Columba, Claudel . . . When shall we have time for Sedulius, Prudentius, and Venantius Fortunatus, for Teresa and John of the Cross, for Léon Bloy and Péguy and Maritain? Then there is that incredibly beautiful literature, written, for the most part anonymously, out of Christian hearts in every age and enshrined in the Missal, the Breviary, the Ritual; it verifies, one sometimes thinks, more than any other literature the definition St. Augustine gave of beauty: *Splendor veri*—truth radiant and shining.

We have called these lectures "The Candlemas Lectures," and decided to have them annually on Candlemas Day. Before Mass on Candlemas morning, the Church, according to immemorial rite, blesses and presents candles to her children, as symbols of Christ, the true Light which enlighteneth every man. Prudentius, the Christian poet of the fourth century, says in his *Hymn for the Lighting of Lamps* that human souls receive the light of grace and the fire of charity from the spark struck off the cornerstone which is Christ, and the Church on this day prays that as these lighted candles drive off the darkness of night, so Christ may drive away from our hearts the darkness of infidelity and sin. St. Paul, writing to the Ephesians, had said the same thing: "Awake, thou that sleepest, and arise from the dead, and Christ shall give thee light." It is the Person of Christ who is central to this wealth of literature, and it is the doctrines of Christ, impinging on responsive or rebellious human hearts, which form its content. We feel that lectures on Christian Literature are aptly named for Him who has en-

11

lightened us and our fathers in the Faith, when we might otherwise have sat in darkness and in the shadow of death.

We feel that we were most fortunate in being able to bring to Boston for the inauguration of these lectures Father Alexander Denomy, of the Congregation of St. Basil. Father Denomy is already known as a scholar whose abiding interest for many years has been mediaeval literature. A Canadian, he had taken his degree at the University of Western Ontario before coming to Harvard for his doctorate. He has spent considerable time in Europe and particularly at the Sorbonne. Since 1935 he has been Professor of the History of Comparative Literature at the Pontifical Institute of Mediaeval Studies at Toronto. He has contributed many articles to the scholarly journal, *Mediaeval Studies,* and is now managing editor of that periodical. His book, *The Old French Lives of St. Agnes,* was published in 1938 as one of the Harvard Studies in Romance Languages. Since giving the lecture which follows, he has been awarded a Guggenheim fellowship for research. In inviting him to her campus, Boston College felt that she was recognizing the merit of long years of patient, persevering study for the glory of God, and conferring a deserved honor on a scholar of reputation. She felt also that his appointment honored the institution Father Denomy represents, an institution founded and carried on brilliantly at the cost of much labor and sacrifice by the Basilian Fathers with the cooperation of such men as Etienne Gilson, Gerald B. Phelan, and Anton C. Pegis. But the distinction of the appointment shone both ways, and Boston College was honored in conferring honor.

WILLIAM LANE KELEHER, S.J.
President of Boston College

THE HERESY OF
COURTLY LOVE

THE HERESY OF
COURTLY LOVE

T SEEMS quite normal and natural to us today that love should be looked upon as irresistible, as a noble and ennobling passion. We find nothing abnormal in the portrayal of the woman loved as an exalted creature whose every whim and fancy is to be obeyed and served. We do not find it strange, either, that the content of love poetry and fiction should be the expression of the lover's unfulfilled desires and restless longings, his devotion and humility, his ecstasy of pain and rapture. These are, after all, but commonplaces of modern literature and, to a large extent, of our own way of thinking

It is only when we begin to compare our attitude towards love and the position of women with that of Oriental nations, for example, that we begin to realize

how specialized and how different is our attitude from theirs. There is something engaging and romantic to us in the story of two lovers driven into each other's arms by inexorable, ecstatic love, with or without, as it is so euphemistically put, benefit of clergy. There is an aura of nobility about a man who gives up all for the woman he loves. We feel a certain sympathy, too, for a man or woman who has failed to find the happiness he or she expected to find in marriage and who seeks it covetously and restlessly outside the marriage bonds. We are apt to picture the rapturous delight they think to find as something exalted and glamorous, purging away the dross and routine dullness of ordinary life, opening up the way to a fuller, better life enriched with new experiences.

It is only when we begin to relate all of these to Christian faith and morality that we realize, actually, how alien they are, or rather should be, to us as Christians. It is only when we recall that there are a Sixth and Ninth Commandment, that marriage is indissoluble, that the Christian ideal is one of self-discipline and self-mastery, that the passion of love was instilled by God into the hearts of His creatures primarily for the preservation of the species and not for the abuse of personal sense pleasure; it is only when we try to explain to our-

18

selves the glorification of women in terms of Christian teaching and tradition, that we begin to realize how wide is the chasm that separates our romantic conception of love and Christianity. This paper is an attempt to explain the genesis of that antinomy in its historical background.

Courtly Love is not, strictly speaking, a theme that one might look for in a lecture on Christian literature. It is, if anything, at variance with the Christian teaching and morality that should be reflected there. I have chosen it because, ever since the twelfth century, literature in Christian lands has undergone its insidious and subtle influence. Courtly Love made its appearance in the Middle Ages, in a culture and civilization that were Christian; for that reason, we are inclined to feel that its erotic principles cannot possibly be as opposed to Christianity as their teaching implies. If we have not been able to reconcile them with Christianity, at least we have become inured to them and accept them almost automatically. In that way, they do not do too much violence to our Christian conscience and scruples.

The content of love literature, a great deal of our etiquette that governs the relationship of the sexes, our very conception of romantic love—are an inheritance of the Middle Ages. They derive from an institution that we have come to know as Courtly Love. It was introduced into literature by the troubadours of the South of France in the early decades of the twelfth century. By their literary innovation they erected a barrier between the literature of the classical past, Latin and vernacular literatures contemporary with them, and the literary tradition which followed them in Western Europe. Their conception of love spread quickly into Northern France, into Italy, Spain, England and Germany, and subsequently among those peoples that have come under the influence of the culture and civilization of those countries. It has come down to us in an unbroken tradition that has survived the satire of almost every century, the opposition inspired by the resurgence of the classics and of middle-class and puritan morality.

The novelty of Courtly Love lies in three basic elements: first, in the ennobling force of human love; second, in the elevation of the beloved to a place of superiority above the lover; third, in the conception of love as ever unsatiated, ever increasing desire. Of course, the troubadour lyrics were embellished with other conceits, formulae and situations: the nature introduction, the personification of love as a god with absolute power over his army of lovers, the idea of love

20

as a sickness with all its familiar exterior manifestations, the ceaseless fears of the lover at losing his beloved, at not being worthy of her, at displeasing her, the position of inferiority of the lover and the feeling of timidity to which that feeling gives rise, the capriciousness, haughtiness and disdain of the beloved, the need of secrecy, stealth and furtiveness in the intrigue, the danger of tale-bearers, and so on. These notions and conceits have their parallels and analogues in classical literature, in mediaeval Latin and Arabic love literature. They are not peculiar to Courtly Love, but are, rather, universally human and belong to the general fund of love literature. It is, on the contrary, the three basic elements of the conception of love as desire, the ennobling force of love, and the cult of the beloved that make Courtly Love to be Courtly Love and which set it apart from all other conceptions of love. They provide, as it were, the skeleton framework, the mechanics or thought pattern of Courtly Love: the surge of the lover to rise in worth and in virtue towards the beloved through the force and energy of desire.[1]

It is from these basic principles that flow consequences that are peculiar to and characteristic of Courtly Love. These consequences are, in a way, the mortar and stone of the structure of Courtly Love. Since love is ennobling, since it is the source of all virtue and good, since man is worthless unless he acts under the compulsion of love, there follows the absolute necessity, incumbent on everyone, of practicing love. Bernard de Ventadour is but expressing the dominant thought of the troubadours when he says:

> Per re non es om tan prezans
> com per amor e per domnei,
> que d'aqui mou deportz e chans
> e tot can a proez' abau.
> nuls om ses amor re no vau.[2]

Therefore, since love offers everyone an incentive towards good, since everyone who wishes to have the praise of the world must indulge in love, Courtly Love not only condones fornication, adultery, sacrilege, but represents them as necessary sources of what it calls virtue. It is a grave error to condemn love in maidens, in the married, even in the clergy. Marriage is no bar to love. On the contrary, the married must practice love outside the marriage bonds if husband and wife are to advance in worth. The troubadours recognized the truth of this axiom of Courtly Love by addressing their love lyrics almost exclusively to married women. There is no love between married people because between them there is equality and, therefore, only affection. This feeling can never take the place of love, for it lacks by definition the constituent element of love—desire.[3] Once a woman becomes man's equal in marriage, she ceases to be his goal.

It is desire that is love, the yearning of the vassal lover for his exalted lady. It is not self-torture, stoical self-renunciation practiced for its own sake. It is a love wherein desire is a means towards an end: progress and growth in virtue, merit and worth. Desire is an integral part, an essential part, but what is of the very essence of Courtly Love is its ennobling force, the elevation of the lover effected by a ceaseless desire and yearning for union with a worthy lady. Desire is the means towards the final end of Courtly Love: the ennobling of the lover.[4]

It is this conception of love as desire that is at the basis of what the troubadours have called pure love —true, excellent love. Pure love consists in the union of the hearts and minds of the lovers.[5] It is a love that yearns for and, at times, is rewarded by the solace of every delight of the beloved except the physical possession of her. That is not allowed to those who love purely.[6] The troubadour Daude de Pradas phrases it thus:

> Non sap de dompnei pauc ni pro
> qui del tot vol sidonz aver.
> Non es dompneis, pois torn' a ver,
> ni cors s'i ren per guizerdo.[7]

Rather it is desire and yearning for one's lady that is productive of joy, for thereby is the lover ennobled. The preference given to unfulfilled desire and to the joy of serving a beloved unrequited is a commonplace among the troubadours.[8] Pure love, in this sense, becomes the ideal of Courtly Love.[9] Near the close of the troubadour period in Provençal literature, the poet Uc Brunec laments the passing of this type of love, longs for the pure love of yesteryears and states that love dies with fulfillment:

> Que sazos fon, que'l maior don d'amar
> Voli' om mais esperar que aver;
> Et eras vey qued az emplit voler
> Moro'l dezir, que solon dous nafrar.
> Per que val mais d'amor so qu'om n'aten,
> Que'l cochos don desavinen no fan,

24

Que'l mals n'es bos e plazentier l'afan,
E'l sospir dous, e'l maltrag iauzimen.[10]

Far from being pure in the accepted sense or dis-
interested, pure love is sensual, carnal and selfish in
that it allows, approves and encourages all that fans
and provokes desire. Despite all the sensuality that
such loves implies, for the troubadours it was a spiritual
love in that it sought a union of hearts and minds and
not of bodies. It was a virtuous love in so far as it was
the source of all good and virtue:

> *Ben devon li amador*
> *De bon cor servir Amor,*
> *Quar amors non es peccatz*
> *Anz es vertutz quels malvatz*
> *Fai bos, elh bo'n son melhor,*
> *E met om en via*
> *De bon far tota dia;*
> *E d'amor mou castitatz*
> *Quar qui'n amor ben s'enten*
> *No pot far que puois mal renh.*[11]

That is Courtly Love. It is neither Christian *caritas*
nor platonic love; it is neither mystical love nor lust,
but a special type of love peculiar to the troubadours

25

by whom, as far as historical texts allow us to know, it was formed, developed and spread. It is a love that is divorced from physical possession, based on the desire for it, practiced by people of worth and regarded as productive of every virtue and every good.[12]

At the opposite pole according to the courtly code is [false love, evil and impure, founded on sensuality for its own sake, faithless, promiscuous and mercenary. Such a love is but a counterfeit of true love, the source of evil, practiced by the wanton, the criminal and the debauched. It reduces man to the level of the beast. By it all that is good and noble, of worth and value in man is brought to naught.] It is against such love that the troubadours inveighed.[13] Not that they condemned the love of physical possession as a source of good. Such love will be called mixed love. It is a love which begins as pure love and terminates in physical union. Because such a love lasts but a short while, because it weakens and lessens desire, may even put an end to it, the practice of pure love was preferred to it. Mixed love, however, was recognized as true love because, like pure love, it proceeds from the same concupiscible feeling of the heart and its substance is the same, that is, desire. Mixed love is true love because it is desire and, as desire, it is productive of every good.[14]

Courtly Love was formed, developed and spread in a milieu that was fundamentally Christian and which had been so for centuries. The lyrics that voice the sentiments of Courtly Love were written by men who were, for the most part, Christians and who had been reared in that faith and in that atmosphere. Aside from a purely surface coloring and the transference of the Christian virtues to the lover, there is little or no trace of Christianity in their love lyrics. When the troubadours do refer to God and to holy things, invariably their references strike us as shocking and irreverent.[15] The conception of love they developed is directly at variance with Christian morality. It is impossible to reconcile the tenets of Courtly Love with the commandments of God, with the Divine Will as interpreted by Saint Paul, with the teaching of Christ and of His Church.[16] From the point of view of the troubadours, however, love, illicit and adulterous at least in aspiration though it may be, is the source of all good and of all virtue, even of chastity.

There is no indication, implied or explicit, that the troubadours were conscious of anything shocking, irreverent or disrespectful in invoking the divine assistance and the aid of holy persons and holy things to further their quest for what, in Christian eyes, is sinful and immoral. Likewise, there is no indication that they were conscious of the sinfulness or the immorality of their conception of love, even of their pure love. On the contrary. As a matter of fact, they were not at all concerned with the Christian concept of the morality of human love, at least in their poems. They simply did not advert to it, or, if they did, they ignored it. Courtly Love is neither moral nor immoral. It is amoral in the sense that it is wholly divorced from Christian morality. When we read their lyrics, we are inclined, unconsciously perhaps, to judge their conception of love by a code of morality that is ours. Whether we are conscious of it or not, we apply to Courtly Love criteria of morality that are Christian, standards governing the relationship of the sexes that are derived from Christian principles and Christian teachings. The morality or immorality of Courtly Love for those who taught it rests not on the commandments of God, the teaching of Christ or of His Church, but simply in this: Does love further a man in virtue or does it effect a regress; does it ennoble him or degrade him?[17]

How, then, account for such a teaching in a Christian society? No Christian teaching could give rise to such a conception of love nor could Christianity ever countenance such a love as the source of all good and

all virtue. Nor is it pagan in origin. The pagan conception of love would recognize the pleasures and delights to be derived from sensual desires and indulgence;
it would never provide the basis for a dogma that such
carnal desires fanned by sensual delights ennobled man
and was the fount of virtue. Ovid, for instance, never
claimed that such love is ennobling; he would admit
that it was shameful and debasing.[18] The heresy of
the Albigensians has often been pointed out as the basis
of Courtly Love. But the teachings of Courtly Love
are incompatible, too, with its tenets.[19] Passion and
sensual pleasures were considered evil and sinful, the
work of the Prince of Evil. The Arabians had a certain
conception of pure love. Ibn Dawoud taught it in his
Book of the Flower,[20] Ibn Hazm described it in detail
in his *Dove's Neck-Ring*[21] and the children of the myth-
ical Bedouin tribe, the Banou Odhrah, practiced it.[22]
It was a love of desire that remained desire that love
might endure. It remained pure in spite of the sensual
delights that accompanied it. But it was not considered
as the fount and origin of virtue and, because of that,
it lacks the very essence of Courtly Love.

The origin of the courtly conception of love as
ennobling is to be found not in Arabian literature but,
rather, in Arabian philosophy and specifically in the

mystical philosophy of Avicenna. In his *Treatise on Love*, Avicenna treats of the love of external beauty.[23] He assigns to human love, the love of the sexes, a positive and contributory role in the ascent of the soul to divine love and union with the divine. Hitherto, Arabian philosophy and mysticism had distinguished sharply between the animal and rational souls in man and had separated distinctly the orbits of their activity into natural and spiritual love. Man's destiny was to seek the highest beauty and this was solely the work of the rational soul. External beauty, though deriving from the beauty of the soul, belonged to nature and was the object of natural love. Love of external beauty, the love of man for woman, had a good in itself, that is, unification with the object loved, but that love remained an activity of the animal soul. Attraction to external beauty, therefore, was regarded as an impediment and obstacle to the soul's ascent to the divine in so far as it turned the rational soul away from its real good, spiritual beauty. It was to be suppressed and wholly mortified.[24]

Avicenna, on the contrary, assigned to the lower soul a role of partnership with the rational soul whereby love of external beauty, sexual love, served as an aid in approaching the divine. Joined to the rational soul, the animal soul gained in excellence and nobility through its alliance with the higher faculty. In this state and condition it pursued sense pleasure with a fine, less gross intention so that its very actions were similar to those of the rational soul. Desire for union with external beauty, the beloved, therefore, is more than a yearning for voluptuous pleasure; it becomes a means of furthering the rational soul along its journey to the Supreme Good. The conditions demanded in this alliance are submission of the animal soul to the rational soul on the one hand, and the domination of the rational soul over the animal soul on the other. The powers of the lower soul must be governed by moral virtue and thus subjected and reduced to the status of a tool in the service of the rational soul.[25]

For Avicenna, the morality of human love does not rest on religious or legal grounds; corporal pleasure even in this life is taught by the Law and revealed by Mohammed. The morality of human love rests entirely on the free exercise of the rational soul by which man is furthered along towards union with the absolute Good. The norm of morality is man's progress towards or regress from it. That love, therefore, is noble, a source of nobility, of progress in virtue which is spiritual in intention because, in loving a creature in this fashion,

31

love brings man closer to the source of all virtue.[26] That love is false and degrading which springs only from a sensual intention and animal desire because it harms the rational soul of man, diverts it from its end and impairs its exercise because of the domination over it of the animal soul.[27] Provided, therefore, that sense pleasures do not lead to actions that belong to the animal soul alone, they are quite legitimate, the more so since they become instruments to effect an ever closer union of heart and soul in which true love consists.[28] This love brings the lover closer to the source of all beauty and to the first object of all love, makes him resemble the noblest and most exalted of all beings and results in grace of character, progress in virtue and increase in nobility.[29]

Once having discovered the specific source of the troubadour conception of love in a mystical philosophy that was heretical, how may one account for its acceptance by poets and by a world that was Christian? It does not help to say that they were not aware of the antinomy that lies between Courtly Love and Christian morality.[30] The chasm that lies between them is too deep and too unbridgable for it not to be immediately apparent. Nor can it be said that the troubadours were bad Christians, irreligious and morally evil. A good number of them were so, perhaps, but the majority were average Christians, the products of Christian monastic schools. A few were better than average if one may judge by their later histories. Some, among them Bernard de Ventadour, ended their lives as monks in various monasteries; others became high Church dignitaries—one an abbot, another a bishop, another a Pope. There is no evidence that they were, as a class, oblivious of God, contemptuous of His Church and holy things. Many of them took part in the Crusades; many of them, too, wrote religious verse along with their love lyrics. In the circumstances, it is strange and unnatural that they should conceive of a love as a source of good which, for Christians, was sinful and that they should exalt such a love. It is easy to see how an individual poet or even how several should do so; it is not so easy to understand how a succession of poets should adopt such ideas and ideals and have them codified into a veritable and rigid system and philosophy of life.

It is just in this connection that the *De Amore libri tres* of Andreas Capellanus, the textbook, so to speak, of Courtly Love, assumes its role as one of the important books of the Middle Ages. It makes clear how a world and a civilization that was Christian was able to conceive of a love that was sinful and shameful as the source of good and virtue. It explains the antinomy between Courtly Love and Christianity, not in terms of reconciliation and compromise—they are basically irreconcilable—but as they might exist side by side, each within its own sphere: the mundane alongside the spiritual, the natural alongside the supernatural, the temporal alongside the eternal, the philosophical alongside the theological. As such, it merits some analysis.

Andreas wrote his treatise sometime between 1174-1186, near the close of the Golden Age of the troubadours. Its first two books, the *De Amore* proper, set forth the constituent elements of Courtly Love, its rules and conventions, the art and technique to be employed by lovers for the successful fruition of their love, the errors and vices to be avoided by them that their love may never fail but ever increase. The *De Amore* is followed by a third book, the *De Reprobatione Amoris,* the retraction and rejection of Courtly Love as evil and as the source of evil. It teaches the avoidance of women as weak and vicious, the cultivation of the love of God as the sole source of virtue and good.

The *De Amore* teaches a love that is of this world, a love that is of the earth, earthy. The god of love rules this world.[31] He rewards those who serve him with the choicest gifts of his kingdom; he punishes those who refuse to love with unutterable torments.[32] Human love is the cause and font of all virtue.[33] But those virtues are not the theological virtues of faith, hope and charity, not the supernatural moral virtues, but the purely natural virtues so coveted and prized by the troubadours and courtly lovers: *cortesia, proeza, mesura, pretz, valors, jovens.* As the source of these, love is the most desirable thing in this world[34] and worldly beatitude consists in loving and desiring one's beloved.[35] To serve her is to reign in this world, for thence is the lover's title to the glory of this life.[36]

The method Andreas adapts to show the necessity of love, its supremacy as the origin of all worldly excellence, the desirability of it as the beatitude of this life is that of rational argument: *philosophica consideratio.*[37] The key to his whole method is expressed in the answer made by the man of the higher nobility to the plebeian woman who had refused him her love: "In the present case there is no help for me but to argue with you at length and by discussing the matter find out whether or not it is right for you to deny me your love."[38] The series of dialogues in which the greater part of the *De Amore* is set is a chain of arguments in which Andreas strives to prove the theses of Courtly Love and to refute the objections to them advanced by the woman. Invariably, the man appeals to the reasonableness of his case, to the truth inherent in the matter.

The basis of his doctrine is the nature of things, particularly the nature of man. It belongs to the very nature of man that he should love. Love is a thing that copies nature.[39] Just as nature is common to all men, so love is common to all men without exception.[40] Just as it is wrong to oppose nature, so it is morally wrong not to love. This irresistibility of nature justifies for Andreas the love of clerics. To love is natural and the cleric remains a man by his very nature.[41] It is this irresistibility of nature, too, that provides Courtly Love with a sort of natural morality. Whatever is done under the impulse and compulsion of nature cannot be classed as a sin; it is not right to class as a sin what is natural to man.[42] But what is contrary to nature is forbidden in love and such love lasts but a short while;[43] a defect of nature puts a complete end to love.[44] Andreas insists that the nature of which he speaks is not that which we have in common with the animals.[45] Otherwise, the wanton, the promiscuous might love; even peasants.[46] It is rational nature which sets man apart from the animal that love ennobles, bedecks with virtue and excellence.[47]

By reason and by nature Andreas proves that love is the greatest good in the world, that it constitutes earthly felicity and beatitude, that it is the font and origin of all good. In the *De Reprobatione* he tears down the whole structure he had erected by reason and by nature in the *De Amore*. He replaces it with the Christian conception of man as a supernatural creature, a child of God by grace, with an end wholly different from the natural beautitude he had proposed.[48] In this book, Andreas takes the very opposite tack to show that human love is evil, loathsome and sordid, that women, by their very nature, are weak, infected with every human frailty and vice.[49] Bodily purity and fleshly abstinence, however, are things that every man should have in the presence of God and of men.[50] He should preserve them by all means because, if they are neglected, no good in a man can be completely perfect: "No man, so long as he devotes himself to the service of love, can please God by any other works, even if they are good ones."[51]

These, then, are the two points of view that Andreas set himself to present in his little book.[52] The first point of view is true, if man is viewed as a purely natural and rational creature, subject only to the laws of nature and to the conclusions of reason. The second point of view is true, if man is considered as a supernatural creature subject to divine authority, the only authority valid over him. Andreas interprets Scripture to show that God hates and in both Testaments commands the punishment of those whom He sees engaging in the works of Venus outside the bonds of wedlock or caught in the toils of passion.[53] By such love, our neighbor is injured, whom, according to the divine authority, we are bound to love as ourselves.[54] The same divine authority, he declares, shows that there is no more serious sin than adultery[55] and Scripture shows that love provides for all lovers that heritage which is situated in the exterior darkness.[56] The devil is the author of love and lechery; God, the fountainhead and origin of chastity and modesty.[57] It is human love which wickedly breaks up marriage and turns a husband from his wife.[58] In His law, God forbade the husband to separate from his wife and commanded her that, forsaking all others, she cleave to her husband and be one in flesh with him.[59]

On rational grounds, Andreas proves in the *De Amore* that human love is the most desirable thing in this world, that it is the source of all that is good and of worth here below. In the *De Reprobatione,* in presenting the case of Christian morality against illicit and adulterous love, Andreas appeals to Scripture and to divine authority. Reason and nature demand that man enroll in the army of the god of love, that he seek the pleasures of the flesh that so he might be ennobled and grow in virtue and in worth. The teaching of God and Holy Church, the doctrine of the Fathers, demand that he set aside all human love and seek the love of God alone. In the *De Amore* we are exclusively on the level of reason and human nature; in the *De Reprobatione,* on that of faith and grace. Thus, there is built up an opposition between the *De Amore* and the *De Reprobatione,* between the rational and natural teaching of the former and the theological and supernatural teaching of the latter. In them is seen erected an opposition between nature and grace, between reason and faith, between philosophy and theology. What Andreas teaches to be true according to nature and reason, he teaches to be false according to grace and divine authority. Thus emerges in his work the doctrine of the so-called "double truth."

It was just for that reason and because it taught doctrines that were morally evil that Andreas' treatise was condemned *nominatim* by Bishop Stephen Tempier of Paris on March 7, 1277.[60] Besides being itself condemned for teaching "manifest and execrable errors,"[61] the *De Amore* was grouped together in the condemnation levelled against those "who say that things may be true according to philosophy but not according to Faith, just as if there were two contradictory truths."[62] This was, of course, the "double truth" of the Latin Averroists.

In general, Latin Averroism may be described as the reception of the entirety of the works of Aristotle as commented upon by Averroes and accepted by Latin philosophers sometime about the year 1230. More especially, Latin Averroism comprises a fund of basic doctrines, such as the eternity of the world and the mortality of the soul, which are in opposition to Christian teaching and to sound philosophy.[63] One has but to glance through the 219 propositions condemned at Paris in 1277 to be aware of the range of these theses in natural and moral philosophy, in psychology, logic, theology. Under that wide divergence, the attitude remains the same, for Latin Averroism is characterized not so much by a set of formal doctrines or by a system of philosophy as by an attitude of mind: veneration for Aristotle as the expression of the highest truth accessible

40

to man and the divorce of philosophy from religion and the teaching of faith.[64]

The introduction of Averroism into the Christian Latin world shattered the unity of faith and reason that had existed among philosophers and theologians in a way that earlier Avicennianism had not succeeded in doing. Up to that time, there had been but one outlook on life and the world and that had been a Christian one. Belief and knowledge had been integrated into a well ordered body of knowledge in which the rights of the natural and of the supernatural were both respected. The highest use of man's reason was to serve faithfully the divine revelation and to develop the natural and the supernatural in the light of the supernatural. The harmony of faith and reason was assured because it rested ultimately on the authority of revelation and creation.[65]

Now the Christian thinker was brought face to face with a purely rational outlook upon the universe and the Aristotle of Averroes was accepted as the highest expression of that rational view. In the clash of reason and faith, contradictions soon became evident between the conclusions of reason and the teaching of Revelation, between reason and faith. There were those who, when faced with that incompatibility, were unable or refused to reconcile them; rather, they accepted the Aristotle of Averroes as the highest expression of human reason and deliberately separated the domain of faith from that of reason. Christians of the thirteenth century, the Latin Averroists, deliberately separated philosophy and theology and invoked the former exclusively for all that pertained to pure reason. They accepted as necessary the results of philosophical speculation, but as Christians they believed as true what Revelation taught them. They felt that there was no contradiction between them, provided they be kept separate. It was not, as Gilson has remarked,[66] a mere incident, but a permanent rupture that was to extend into the fourteenth century, beyond the rationalism of the Renaissance into our own day. For it is axiomatic that as often as reason is withdrawn from the jurisdiction of faith, just so often is the temporal withdrawn totally from the jurisdiction of the spiritual. Such an attitude led inevitably to the divorce of almost every department of human endeavor from religion. To establish the independence of reason from faith, that philosophical truth is quite other than religious truth, resulted in a sort of scepticism wherein the tendency was to regard man as a purely rational creature quite apart from his status as a child of God destined to a supernatural end. It has resulted in an attitude that religion has no place in affairs that are purely human — in education, politics, government, ethics, philosophy, and so on.

The expression "double truth," the general tag applied to the teaching of the Latin Averroists, is not a happy one.[67] There must have been Averroists before 1277 who did teach the existence of two simultaneous and contradictory truths and who sided with philosophy against theology just as, for example, Jean de Jandun did in the fourteenth century. Otherwise, the condemnation of 1277 would not have condemned that attitude so specifically, nor would it have included the following among the condemned propositions: There are no wisdoms in the world except that of philosophers;[68] nothing should be believed, save only that which is either self-evident, or can be deduced from self-evident propositions;[69] Christian revelation is an obstacle to learning;[70] theology rests upon fables.[71] Nor would St. Thomas Aquinas have attacked their teachings as he did. Such Averroists did not write or, if they did, their writings have been lost. The expression "double truth" is really the *reductio ad absurdum* made by theologians who were orthodox against philosophers who were not; it simply expresses the declaration of the factual divorce between Revelation and reason.[72]

Siger de Brabant (1235?-1281-84) was one of the masters of Latin Averroism of the thirteenth century against whom the condemnation of 1277 was especially directed. His method of procedure is interesting, in so far as it is also that of Andreas. Siger's position is this: The teaching of Aristotle, which is philosophy, often contradicts Revelation. Reason proves often the contrary to what faith teaches. Then there exist two conclusions on certain questions: One is that of Revelation which is true; the other arises necessarily from philosophy and natural reason.[73] When such a conflict appears, then I can simply say that here are the conclusions to which my reason has led me as a philosopher.[74] But Revelation teaches otherwise and, since God cannot lie, then I adhere to the truth that He has revealed and I cling to it by faith.[75] There is no doubt that Siger, as a philosopher, spoke otherwise than he did as a Christian. His aim as a philosopher was to expound Aristotle; that was philosophy for him. But, if a conflict arose, then as a Christian he could not allow those conclusions that were necessary to prevail against the truth of faith which was infallible. He was content to indicate the conclusions to which philosophy led him and to affirm, on the contrary, the superiority of Revelation. In conflict, it was not reason, but faith, which prevailed.[76]

After all, that is exactly the procedure of Andreas Capellanus. The *De Amore* is the exposition of the conclusions to which natural reason has led him in the realm of the relation of the sexes. The *De Reprobatione*, on the other hand, is the recognition of the direct opposition of these conclusions to the teaching of faith and the expression of his preference for the latter. There is nothing in the expressions he uses to indicate that he was doubtful of the real teaching of faith in regard to human love. Never did he write of Christian faith as if he did not count himself among the partisans of that faith. In the *De Amore* he was writing and thinking as a philosopher; in the *De Reprobatione* he wrote as a Christian, and there is never any doubt on his real stand in these matters. There is no contradiction in maintaining that certain conclusions do necessarily arise from philosophy and certain others from faith and Revelation, if it is expressly admitted that these conclusions to which reason has led him are false. And that is exactly what Andreas did.[77] There is no more reason to question his sincerity than there is to question that of Siger in the realm of philosophy.

Dante had no doubt of Siger's sincerity nor of his faith, although he proceeded exactly as had Andreas Capellanus. Dante placed Siger in the fourth heaven of the Sun, together with St. Albert the Great and St. Thomas Aquinas.[78] He placed him there because Siger had taught certain doctrines dear to him: that philosophy is a science of natural reason and that theology has no authority over natural morality nor on politics which are founded on natural morality.[79] To Dante, Siger represented the divorce of philosophy from theology, of reason from faith, a divorce that he utilized in the political doctrine of the *De Monarchia*. Dante was the first to have put to use in politics the characteristic trait of Latin Averroism.[80] His *De Monarchia* is the projection of the separation of reason and faith in the political sphere[81] even as the *De Amore* is the projection of the separation in the moral sphere.

It is quite clear whence arose the characteristic of Latin Averroism: namely, the separation of theology and philosophy, apparent in the philosophical field in Siger de Brabant and Jean de Jandun and in the polit-

46

ical, possibly in Dante and certainly in Marsilius of Padua. But with the *De Amore* we are faced with the peculiar fact that a work that teaches the same separatism in the sphere of ethics was written some forty or fifty years before the advent of the commentaries of Averroes into the Christian Latin world, by a man who was roughly contemporary with Averroes. The solution lies, it seems to me, in this: the teaching of Averroes is simply the definitive form of an attitude common to some Arabian philosophers in regard to theology that existed from the very beginning in Islam. Whereas the Latin Averroists had undergone the direct influence of that attitude as reflected in the commentaries of Averroes on Aristotle, Andreas Capellanus and the troubadours had undergone the influence of the predecessors of Averroes who had professed much the same veneration for Aristotle and the same attitude towards philosophy as the highest truth. As a matter of fact, it is Gautier's thesis that the teaching of Averroes and his attitude are common to all the great Arabian philosophers who had preceded him.[82]

From the very beginning there had existed in Islam a cleavage between its theology and philosophy, between what had been revealed and the conclusions of reason. The philosophy taken over by the Arabs was in reality a synthesis of Aristotle and Plato. Aristotle was their great master, but it was an Aristotle deformed and interpreted according to neoplatonic pantheism and mysticism. On the other hand, there was the *Koran*. Between these two there was the problem of how to think as Aristotle and to believe as Mohammed. On the one hand, there was the strict monotheism of Islam, founded on revelation which taught that reason of itself is incapable of discovering truths of the transcendent order or the sources of moral precepts; on the other, a pantheistic, mystical philosophy, founded on the conclusions of reason.[83] Although as good Muslems their philosophy strove for a reconciliation with dogma, the conclusions to which reason led them were often at odds with orthodoxy. In their systems of philosophy there is a continual internal conflict between faith and reason which amounts to an effort at elucidation never quite completed.[84] It is seen especially in their theory of prophecy with which is connected the question of divine truth,[85] and in their heterodox mysticism which was intellectual and philosophical.[86]

As a result, the Arabian philosophers made use of an esoteric and exoteric doctrine, the first destined to their most faithful and closest followers in which there was a hidden meaning often at variance with orthodoxy.

The latter was destined for common consumption as the philosopher's official teaching and was usually orthodox.[87] It was in reality a sort of "double truth" that foreshadowed Averroes, namely, that there was an official theological truth and at the same time a secret heterodox philosophical truth reserved for the learned and wise, able to distinguish between the true and the false, but forbidden to common humanity. In the preface to the second part of his *Indications and Annotations,* Avicenna writes: "This book contains indications on the basic notions of metaphysics and annotations on its propositions. He only who is endowed with the necessary aptitude may study it, while he who is deprived of that aptitude may draw no profit from it. That is why I repeat my last will and prayer that the contents of this book be hidden from every reader who has not the necessary qualifications."[88] At the conclusion of his book he indicates those to whom it will be safe to reveal his teaching: the trustworthy man free from every evil influence and favored with the light of illumination, grace and the desire for truth.[89]

In much the same fashion as Averroes, his predecessors had looked upon Aristotle and on Plato as philosophy itself, as the expression of the highest truth accessible to human reason. Their veneration for Aristotle and for Plato differed from that of Averroes only in degree, if it differed at all. Their attitude towards philosophy as productive of absolute truth, as leading to conclusions that are necessary, while not as clear-cut as that of Averroes, does not differ in its essentials from his. Thus, if the teaching of these predecessors, Al-Farabi and Avicenna especially, was to reach the Christian Latin world, the world of Andreas Capellanus and that of the troubadours in particular, would it not be plausible that it had the same effects there as that of Averroes had later, say, on Siger de Brabant? There is no positive documentary evidence that it did before the year 1130, when Avicenna was translated. There is no evidence save in the attitude of the troubadours towards Courtly Love and in the *De Amore* of Andreas Capellanus. There the effects of such an influence are as visible as they are later on in Latin Averroism. Identity of effect argues identity of cause. Such an attitude of mind, the supremacy of reason and the separation of reason from faith, arising from a knowledge of Aristotle and deriving originally from Arabian philosophy and mysticism, could have reached the South of France through channels and over bridges that have often been rehearsed: commerce, Crusade, pilgrimage, through Muslim Spain—in short, through contacts of every kind between Arab and Christian.[90]

If it be true that the troubadours and Andreas got their conception of what they called pure love from Avicenna, as I think they did;[91] if it be true that a great number of the formulae and conceits they used were taken over from Arabian love lyrics, as it is held;[92] if it be true that certain verse forms used by the early troubadours were borrowings or adaptations from Arabic verse, as it is certain;[93] then it can be just as true that the troubadours were acquainted with Greek philosophy through the Arabs and the attitude of mind it engendered among them. The influence of Avicenna's *Treatise on Love* appears in their courtly conception of pure love; that of their poetry, in the verse form of Guillaume IX and Marcabru; that of their love lyrics, in a communality of conceits; that of their rational philosophy, in the troubadours' ability to conceive on rational grounds and in the face of the tenets of their faith of a doctrine that human love is the font of virtue and the beatitude of this life. That influence enabled them to reach conclusions that are necessary in the sphere of ethics, as it did later the Latin Averroists in the field of philosophy and politics. It enabled them to see how a thing might be necessary according to reason, but false according to faith, how love might be the origin of all good according to the necessary conclusions of natural reason, but evil and sinful according to the laws of God as well as of the Church.

I think we can understand now why Andreas added the *De Reprobatione* to his *De Amore*.[94] At least he did not add it because, as it is so often claimed, it was demanded by the general scheme of Ovid's *Ars Amatoria* and the *Remedia Amoris*.[95] There is nothing in common between the work of Ovid and that of Andreas. The *Remedia* is not a retraction; it is just what its title signifies: remedies, reliefs from love. Ovid attempts to induce indifference rather than aversion to love and the measures that he prescribes are often no less debasing and demoralizing than the passion itself. The medicine is often worse than the cure.[96] Andreas wrote the *De Reprobatione* for the same reason that Siger de Brabant expressed his firm adherence to the doctrines of faith as often as the conclusions to which reason led him appeared to be in direct opposition to them. Like Siger, Andreas saw that the conclusions he had arrived at through reason in the *De Amore* were opposed to faith and therefore he wrote the *De Reprobatione*. As a good Christian he wished to put himself on the side of orthodoxy. There is no more reason to suspect his sincerity or, even, his orthodoxy than there is to suspect those of Siger. The *De Reprobatione* is, as it were, Andreas' profession of faith in the face of a heresy to which the necessary conclusions of reason had led him.[97]

The *De Reprobatione* is exactly what its title means: the rejection, disapproval, condemnation of Courtly Love. It was called forth, not by any general Ovidian scheme, but by the very nature and subject matter of the *De Amore:* that human love constitutes the happiness of this life and that every worldly good and virtue proceeds from it. His *De Reprobatione* sprang from his clear perception of the utter incompatibility of this doctrine with the tenets of Christian morality and faith, that, in short, it was heretical both from the point of view of content and from that of the method which led to the conclusions he had set down.

He wrote his *De Reprobatione* for the same reason that Chrétien de Troyes some few years before had written his *Perceval,* the *De Reprobatione,* if you will, of the *Lancelot.* The *De Amore,* the official treatise of Courtly Love, is Courtly Love in theory; the *Lancelot,* Courtly Love in practice. The *matière* that Chrétien received from Marie de Champagne and which he incorporated at her behest into the *Lancelot* coincides with the *matière* of the *De Amore:* the extra-conjugal nature of love and the service of love as the means of ennoblement in the eyes of the beloved. [98] Chrétien left the *Lancelot* unfinished, it is claimed, in distaste and disgust; but he did write a *Perceval*, a romance whose central theme is not Courtly Love nor the quest for natural worth and happiness through love, but, on the contrary, a romance of the supernatural life in its quest for God and the things of God under the guise of allegory. There is a curious parallel between the *De Amore* and the *De Reprobatione* on the one hand, and the *Lancelot* and the *Perceval* on the other. I suggest that Andreas and Chrétien, roughly contemporary, writing at the same court and under the direction of Marie, were both motivated by their insight into the incompatibility of Courtly Love with Christian teaching; that the *Perceval* is a repudiation of Courtly Love in favor of divine love in just the same way and in the same measure that the *De Reprobatione* is Andreas' repudiation of his *De Amore*.

Certainly, Andreas wrote his *De Reprobatione* for the same reason that Chaucer wrote the palinode to his *Troilus and Cressida,* the expression of his revulsion as a Christian at the principles of Courtly Love portrayed in the story of these two lovers.[99] It is more than a renunciation of Courtly Love in favor of heavenly love. As Professor Young has pointed out, it is a clear repudiation of it in favor of the love of God.[100] Chaucer saw just as clearly as Chrétien de Troyes and Andreas had before him that the teaching of Courtly Love was immoral and heretical in that it regarded man as a purely natural creature. As Christians, they looked upon man as a supernatural creature, and that quite inseparable from his status as a rational creature. It was not necessary that Chaucer know the *De Amore* or the *De Reprobatione;* all that was necessary was that he be a Christian able to discern the true from the false, the orthodox from the heretical—and that he make choice between them.

NOTES

NOTES

[1]Cf. A. J. Denomy, "An Inquiry into the Origins of Courtly Love," *Mediaeval Studies* VI (1944), especially pp. 175-187.

[2]By nothing is man made so worthy as by love and the courting of women, for thence arise delight and song and all that pertains to excellence. No man is of value without love. *Bernard von Ventadorn, seine Lieder,* ed. Carl Appel (Halle, 1915), 21, 25-32, pp. 119-120. Cf. also, 2, 15-16, p. 11; 42, 5-7, p. 241.

[3]Vehementer tamen admiror, quod maritalem affectionem quidem, quam quilibet inter se coniugati adinvicem post matrimonii copulam tenentur habere, vos vultis amoris sibi vocabulum usurpare, quum liquide constet inter virum et uxorem amorem sibi

locum vindicare non posse. Licet enim nimia et immoderata affectione coniungantur, eorum tamen affectus amoris non potest vice potiri, quia nec sub amoris verae definitionis potest ratione comprehendi. Quid enim aliud est amor nisi immoderata et furtivi et latentis amplexus concupiscibiliter percipiendi ambitio? Sed quis esse possit, quaeso, inter coniugatos furtivus amplexus, quum ipsi se adinvicem possidere dicantur et cuncta sine contradictionis timore suae voluntatis desideria vicissim valeant adimplere? *Andreae Capellani de Amore libri tres,* ed. Amadeu Pagès (Castelló de la Plana, 1930), p. 83; tr. John Jay Parry, *The Art of Courtly Love* (New York, 1941), p. 100.

[4]It is not the beloved that ennobles the lover, but the love of her:

> *Ja non creirai, qui que m'o jur,*
> *Que vins non iesca de razim,*
> *Et hom per Amor no meillur;*
> *C'anc un pejurar non auzim,*
> *Qu'ieu vaill lo mais per la meillor.*

Poésies complètes du troubadour Marcabru, ed. J. M. L. Dejeanne (Toulouse, 1909), XIII, 25-29, p. 54.

Cf. also *Les Poésies de Cercamon,* ed. Alfred Jeanroy (Paris, 1922), V, 7-10, p. 15; Bernard de Ventadour, *ed. cit.,* 24, 17-24, p. 140.

[5]*En agradar et en voler*
es l'amors de dos fis amans.

Bernard de Ventadour, *ed. cit.,* 15, 29-30, p. 86.

[6]Et purus quidem amor est, qui omnimoda dilectionis affectione duorum amantium corda coniungit. Hic autem in mentis contemplatione cordisque consistit affectu; procedit autem usque ad oris osculum lacertique amplexum et verecundum amantis nudae contactum, extremo praetermisso solatio; nam illud pure amare volentibus exercere non licet. *De Amore,* pp. 105-106; Parry, p. 122.

[7]He knows little or nothing of the service of women who wishes to possess his lady entirely. That is not the service of women when such becomes a reality, nor does one yield one's heart for the sake of reward. *Poésie de Daude de Pradas,* ed. A. H. Schutz (Toulouse, 1933), XIV, p. 71.

⁸Bona dompna de totz bos aips complida,
tant etz valens part las meillors qu'ieu sai,
mais am de vos lo talen e'l desir
que d'autr' aver tot so c'a drut s'eschai.

*Les Poésies lyriques du troubadour Arnaut de Ma-
reuil,* ed. R. C. Johnston (Paris, 1935), p. 45.

⁹The troubadour Folquet de Marseilles witnesses its
general acceptance and attests the judgment of com-
petent judges as to its worth:

Et es ben dregz, qu'al laus dels conoissens
es plus valens;
Per qu'ieu n'am mas l'afan
De lieys servir que d'autr' aver joi gran.

Le Troubadour Folquet de Marseille, ed. Stanislaw
Stronski (Cracow, 1919), XXI, 13-16, pp. 92-93.

¹⁰There was a time when one preferred to hope for
rather than to have the greatest gift of love. Now I
see that those desires which used to wound so sweetly
die with the fulfilment of the will. Wherefore, what
one hopes for from love is of more value than its hasty,
obnoxious gifts, for the pain that arises from it is

good, pleasant the toil, sweet the longings and the suffering joy. Ed. Carl Appel, "Der Trobador Uc Brunet," *Abhandlungen Herrn. Prof. Dr. Adolf Tobler* (Halle, 1896), pp. 75-76.

[11]Lovers ought, indeed, to serve love gladly, for love is not a sin. Rather it is a virtue which makes the evil good and through it the good become better. It puts man in the way of doing good daily. From love arises chastity because he who turns all his thoughts on love cannot do anything afterwards that is evil. *Le Troubadour Guilhem Montanhagol*, ed. Jules Coulet (Toulouse, 1898), p. 69.

[12]Cf. A. J. Denomy, *"Fin' Amors:* the Pure Love of the Troubadours, its Amorality, and Possible Source," *Mediaeval Studies* VII (1945), pp. 139-179.

[13]The troubadour Marcabru best exemplifies this teaching. He calls this type of love *Amars* in contrast to *bon' amors* or simply *Amors*. The contrast appears clearly in such passages as:

> *Bon' Amors porta meizina*
> *Per garir son compaigno,*
> *Amars lo sieu disciplina*
> *E'l met en perdicio.*

Poésies complètes du troubadour Marcabru, ed. J. M.
L. Dejeanne, XXXI, 28-31, p. 146.

> *Qu'ieu dis e dic e dirai*
> *Quez amors et amars brai,*
> *E qui blasm' Amor buzina.*

Ibid., 78-81, p. 149. Cf. also XXXVI, 13-18, pp. 174-
175; XXXVII, 7-24, pp. 178-179.

[14]Mixtus vero amor dicitur ille, qui omni carnis delec-
tationi suum praestat effectum et in extremo Veneris
opere terminatur . . . . Nam et mixtus amor verus
est amor atque laudandus et cunctorum esse dicitur
origo bonorum. *De Amore,* p. 106; Parry, p. 122.
Licet enim purus et mixtus diversi videantur amores,
recte tamen intuentibus purus amor quo ad sui sub-
stantiam idem cum mixto iudicatur amore et ex
eadem cum ipso cordis affectione procedit. Eadem
est in illis amoris substantia. *Ibid.,* p. 153; Parry, p.
164.

[15]Cf. Victor Lowinsky, "Zum geistlichen Kunstliede in
der altprovenzalischen Literatur bis zum Gründung
des Consistoire del Gai Saber," *Zeitschrift für fran-*

zösische *Sprache und Literatur* XX (1898), pp. 163-165, and A. J. Denomy, "An Inquiry . . .," pp. 181-182.

[16]Cf. Exod. 20:14,17; I Thess. 4:3-5; I Cor. 7:1; I Peter 2:11; II Peter 2:9-14; Matt. 5:27-30.

> [17]*C'Amors a signifianssa*
> *De maracd' o de sardina,*
> *E[s] de Joi cim' e racina,*
> *C'ab veritat seignoreia,*
> *E sa poestatz sobranssa*
> *Sobre mouta creatura.*
>
> *Segon dich, faich e semblanssa,*
> *Es de veraia corina*
> *Car se promet e's plevina,*
> *Ab sol que'l dos ne sordeia,*
> *E qui vas lieis no s'enanssa*
> *Porta nom de follatura.*

Poésies complètes de Marcabru, ed. cit., XXXVII, 31-42, p. 180.

[18]Cf. Willibald Schrötter, *Ovid und die Troubadours* (Halle, 1908): "Ovid sagt Liebe erniedrigt; die Troubadouren sagen Liebe veredelt," p. 48.

[19]Cf. Denis de Rougemont, *L'Amour et l'occident* (Paris, 1939), especially pp. 71-116, and A. J. Denomy, "An Inquiry . . .," p. 258, note 4.

[20]Ed. A. R. Nykl and I. Tuqan (Chicago, 1932). The work is still untranslated. A plan of it and the title of the first fifty chapters are found in Louis Massignon, *La Passion d'Al-Hallaj* (Paris, 1914-21), pp. 170-171.

[21]Tr. A. R. Nykl (Paris, 1931). Cf. *Hispano-Arabic Poetry and Its Relations with the Old Provençal Troubadours* (Baltimore, 1946), pp. 73-103. Cf. also Joseph Hell, "Al-'Abbas ibn al-Ahnaf, der Minnesänger am Hofe Harun ar-Rasid's," *Islamica* II (1926), especially pp. 295 ff.

[22]Cf. Louis Massignon, *The Encyclopedia of Islam,* IV² (London, 1929), *art.* Udhri, p. 990; A. J. Denomy, *Mediaeval Studies* VII (1945), pp. 186-188.

[23]*Risalah fi'l-'Ishq,* ed. M. A. F. Mehren, *Traités mystiques d'Aboû Alî al-Hosain b. Abdallâh b. Sînâ ou d'Avicenne* III*e* fasc. (Leyden, 1894), pp. 1-27. Mehren gives a resume of the content of the treatise. It has been translated into English by Emil L. Facken-

heim, "A Treatise on Love by Ibn Sina," *Mediaeval Studies* VII (1945), pp. 208-228.

[24]Cf. *The Kashf Al-Mahjub, the Oldest Persian Treatise on Sufism by Ali b. 'Uthman al-Jullabi al-Hujwiri,* tr. R. A. Nicholson (London, 1911, Gibb Memorial Volume XVII). The Sufi considered human love as a passion, an attribute of the lower soul, which is the source and principle of evil, pp. 308, 196, 217-209, 360-366. The most important treatment of love in Arabic philosophy prior to Avicenna is found in the Encyclopedia of the Brethren of Purity. There the function of love is to lead men away from sensual and bodily pleasures which belong to the animal soul to the beauty of the spiritual world. Cf. *Die Abhandlungen der Ichwan as-Safa,* ed. F. Dieterici (Leipzig, 1886), pp. 504 ff.; T. J. de Boer, *The Encyclopedia of Islam* II (London, 1927), *art.* Ikhwan as-Safa, pp. 459 ff.

[25]Cf. "A Treatise on Love by Ibn Sina," Chapter V, *On the Love of Those who are Noble-Minded and Young for External Beauty, tr. cit.,* pp. 218-222.

[26]If a man loves a beautiful form with animal desire, he deserves reproof, even condemnation and the

charge of sin. . . . But whenever he loves a pleasing form with an intellectual consideration, in the manner we have explained, then this is to be considered as an approximation to nobility and an increase in goodness. For he covets something whereby he will come nearer to the influence of That which is the First Source of influence and the First Object of love, and more similar to the exalted and noble beings. And this will dispose him to grace, generosity and kindness. *Ibid.,* p. 221.

[27] As for the third [urge for conjugal union], it is obvious that this is specific to the animal soul alone, and its hold on the latter is very strong, so much so that it maintains the position of a steady companion, more, of a master, and certainly not of a tool. It is very hideous. Rational love, therefore, can not be pure except when the animal faculty is altogether subdued. *Ibid.,* pp. 221-222.

[28] As for embracing and kissing, the purpose in them is to come near to one another and to become united. The soul of the lover desires to reach the object of his love with his senses of touch and sight, and thus he delights in embracing it. And he longs to have the very essence of his soul-faculty, his heart mingle with

that of the object of his love, and thus he desires to kiss it. These actions, then, are not in themselves blameworthy. *Ibid*. p. 222.

[29]Whoever is filled with this type of love is a man of nobility and refinement, and this type of love is an ornament and a source of inner wealth. *Ibid*.

[30]One may catch a glimpse of the consciousness of that antagonism that lay between the service of God and the service of women. Guillaume IX, Duke of Aquitaine, the first known troubadour, gives evidence of it:

> *De proeza e de joi fui,*
> *Mais ara partem ambedui;*
> *Et eu irai m'en a scellui*
> *On tut peccador troban fi.*
>
> *Mout ai estat cuendes e gais,*
> *Mas nostre Seigner no'l vol mais;*
> *Ar non puesc plus soffrir lo fais,*
> *Tant soi aprochatz de la fi.*
>
> *Tot ai guerpit cant amar sueill,*
> *Cavalaria et orgueill;*

69

E pos Dieu platz, tot o acueill,
E prec li que'm reteng' am si.

Les Chansons de Guillaume IX, ed. Alfred Jeanroy
(Paris, 1913), XI, 25-36, p. 28. Pierre d'Auvergne
will re-echo Guillaume's farewell to love and the
courtly service of women with the implication that
such love and service are incompatible with the love
and service of God:

Amors, be'us degra doler,
si negus autr' enginhaire
mas lo dreituriers jutjaire
de vos me pogues mover,
que per vos er' enriquitz,
essausatz et enantiz
e pel senher de Belcaire.

Mas so non pot remaner,
cortez' amors de bon aire,
don mi lais esser amaire,
tan m'agrad' er a tener
lai on vol sanhs esperitz;
e mas el mezeis m'es guitz,
no'us pes s'ab vos non repaire.

Die Lieder Peires von Auvergne, ed. Rudolf Zenker (Erlangen, 1900), XV, 50-63, pp. 123-124.

[31]Sed omnes amoris postulantes deservire militiae abiecerunt et tanquam sibi odiosos repulerunt eum non recolentes omnino, qui deus amoris dicitur . . . . per quem universus regitur mundus. *De Amore,* pp. 56-57; Parry, p. 77.

[32]Talem igitur deum non est offendere tutum, sed in omnibus est sibi servire tutissimum, qui talibus suos novit praemiis munerare et suos contemptores tam gravibus poenis affligere. *De Amore,* p. 57; Parry, p. 78.

[33]Nullum in mundo bonum vel curialitas exercetur, nisi ex amoris fonte derivetur. Omnis ergo boni erit amor origo et causa. *De Amore,* p. 15; Parry, p. 40. Nam quum omnibus, quae fiunt in saeculo, bonis amor praestet initium, merito in primis tanquam omnium bonorum radix et causa principalis est postulandus. *De Amore,* p. 38; Parry, p. 61. Quid enim valeat in saeculo bonum ab aliquo exerceri, nisi ex amore suam sumat originem, videre non possum. *De Amore,* p. 49; Parry, p. 71. Quum enim omnis ex amoris rivuli plentitudine procedat urbanitas, eoque magistro omni

benefacto praestetur initium, omnisque exitus boni-
tatis peragatur. . . . *De Amore,* p. 34; Parry, p. 58.
Nam si non liceret hominibus sui, quum vellent, cordis
dominabus aperire secreta, iam amor perisset omnino,
qui omnium dicitur fons et origo bonorum, et nullus
sciret aliis subvenire, omniaque curialitatis opera
hominibus essent ignota. *De Amore,* p. 46; Parry, p.
68. Cf. also, *De Amore,* p. 57; Parry, p. 77. *De Amore,*
p. 106, Parry, p. 122. *De Amore,* p. 97, Parry, p. 114,
etc.

[34]Sed amore in orbe nihil appetibilius reperitur, quum
ex eo omnis boni procedat instructio, et sine eo nihil
boni aliquis operetur in orbe. *De Amore,* p. 50; Parry,
p. 72. Nihil in orbe sedet, quod meus tam avide de-
sideret animus ut evidenter facere possim, quam quod
laudibus sit et praemio dignum. *De Amore,* p. 77;
Parry, p. 95. Res est igitur amor ab omnibus appe-
tenda et a cunctis diligenda per orbem. *De Amore,*
p. 100; Parry, p. 117.

[35]O, si inceperis militare amori, beatus erit ille super
omnibus, quem tuo coronabis amore. *De Amore,* p.
11, Parry p. 37. Sciatis igitur . . . . nihilque me posse
in saeculo isto beare nisi pretiosissimum personae
vestrae thesaurum. *De Amore,* pp. 64-65; Parry, p.

84. Neque mulier neque masculus potest in saeculo beatus haberi nec curialitatem nec aliqua bona perficere, nisi sibi haec fomes praestet amoris. *De Amore,* pp. 69-70; Parry, p. 88. Fateor . . . . prae cunctis in orbe viventibus beatitudinis gaudiis honorari, qui vestrae celsitudinis gaudia suo meruit amplexu percipere. *De Amore,* pp. 82-83; Parry, p. 100. Sine quo [Amor] etiam diu non potest corporali vita beari. *De Amore,* p. 151; Parry, p. 163.

[36]Quod vobis servire solum est cunctis in hac vita regnare, et sine ipso nihil posset ab aliquo in hoc saeculo dignum laudibus adimpleri. *De Amore,* p. 74, Parry, p. 92.

[37]An excellent illustration of his method is seen in a judgment handed down by the Lady Ermengarde of Narbonne on a question submitted to her: whether a greater measure of affection is found between the married or between lovers. Cui eadem domina philosophica consideratione respondit. Ait enim: Maritalis affectus et coamantium vero dilectio penitus iudicantur esse diversa et ex motibus omnino differentibus suam sumunt originem. Et ideo inventio ipsius sermonis aequivoca actus comparationis excludit et sub diversis ea facit speciebus adiungi. Ces-

sat enim collatio comparandi per magis et minus inter res aequivoce sumptas, si ad commune nomen, cuius respectu dicuntur aequivocae, comparatio referatur. Non enim competens esset comparatio talis, si diceretur, nomen corpore simplicius esse vel proposito magis dictione composita. *De Amore,* p. 161; Parry, p. 171.

[38]Parry, p. 88. Ergo mihi nullum in disputatione praesenti reservatur auxilium nisi vobiscum pleno sermone certare atque disputando cognoscere, utrum vos deceat vel non mihi vestrum denegare amorem. *De Amore,* p. 69.

[39]Res est enim amor, quae ipsam imitatur naturam. *De Amore,* p. 20; Parry, p. 45.

[40]Cognosco igitur manifeste, quod amor non consuevit homines discretionis stilo discernere, sed omnes pariter angit in suo, id est, amoris exercitu militare . . . hoc solum discernens, an aliquis sit aptus ad amoris arma ferenda . . . . Sicut igitur uniuscuiusque generis homines amor cogit accendi, ita et amantes non genera discernere debent sed hoc solum, an sit sauciatus amore, qui petit amari. *De Amore,* pp. 19-20; Parry, p. 45. Sine omni contradictione profiteor, quod amor indifferenter cogit amare. *De Amore,* p. 22; Parry,

74

p. 47. Homines universos ex ipso instinctu cupidinis naturaliter in cuiuslibet alterius sexus personae libidinem provocari. *De Amore, ibid;* Parry, *ibid.*

[41]Homo tamen sum in peccatis conceptus et carnis lapsui sicut et ceteri homines naturaliter pronus exsistens. *De Amore,* p. 108; Parry, p. 124. Carnis incentivo naturaliter instigetur sicut et reliqui universi mortales. *De Amore,* p. 109; Parry, p. 125. Videns enim Dominus, suos clericos iuxta humanae naturae infirmitatem in varios lapsuros excessus. *De Amore, ibid.;* Parry, *ibid.*

[42]Credo tamen, in amore Deum graviter offendi non posse; nam quod natura cogente perficitur, facili potest expiatione mundari. Praeterea fas nullatenus esse videtur, id inter crimina reputare, a quo bonum in hac vita summum habet initium, et sine quo nullus in orbe posset laude dignus haberi. *De Amore,* p. 94; Parry, p. 111.

[43]Nam quod ultra cuiusque noscitur pervenire naturam, modica solet aura dissolvi et brevi momento durare. *De Amore,* p. 30; Parry, p. 54. Cf. also, *De Amore,* p. 65; Parry, p. 85.

[44]Si vero ex coamantis delicto procedat vel ipsius naturae defectu, eum aliquando revixisse, memores minime sumus, hoc tamen non impossibile iudicamus nisi forte ubi naturae defectus occurrat. *De Amore,* p. 145; Parry, p. 157.

[45]Istorum talis amor est, qualis est canis impudici. Sed nos credimus asinis comparandos; ea namque solummodo natura moventur, quae ceteris animantibus homines ostendit aequales, non vera, quae rationis differentia nos a cunctis facit animalibus separari. *De Amore,* p. 7; Parry, p. 33.

[46]Dicimus enim vix contingere posse, quod agricolae in amoris inveniantur curia militare, sed naturaliter sicut equus et mulus ad Veneris opera promoventur, quemadmodum impetus eis naturae demonstrat . . . . Sed, etsi quandoque, licet raro, contingat, eos ultra sui naturam amoris aculeo concitari, ipsos tamen in amoris doctrina non expedit erudire, ne, dum actibus sibi naturaliter alienis intendunt, humana praedia . . . nobis facta infructifera sentiamus. *De Amore,* pp. 136-137; Parry, pp. 149-150.

[47]Quantum enim ad partis pertinet inferioris solatia, a brutis in nullo sumus animalibus segregati, sed eis nos

hac parte ipsa natura coniungit. Superioris vera partis solatia tanquam propria humanae sunt attributa naturae et aliis animalibus universis ab ipsa natura negata. Ergo inferioris partis elector tanquam canis ab amore repellatur indignus, et superioris tanquam naturae amplexator admittatur elector. *De Amore*, p. 120; Parry, pp. 135-136.

[48]Cernas ergo, Gualteri, et acuto mentis disquiras ingenio, quanto sit praeferendus honore, qui coelesti rege contempto eiusque neglecto mandato pro mulierculae cuiusdam affectu antiqui hostis non veretur se vinculis alligare . . . . Cuiuslibet igitur hominis satis est admiranda stultitia, qui pro vilissimis Veneris amplectendo terrenis hereditatem amittit aeternam. *De Amore*, p. 182; Parry, p. 188. Quum igitur omnia sequantur ex amore nefanda, nullumque inde bonum evenire cognoscatur sed infinitas hominibus procedere poenas, cur, stulte iuvenis, quaeris amare et te Dei gratia et aeterna hereditate privare? *De Amore*, p. 192; Parry, p. 197.

[49]Nam et mulieres omnes de sexus generali natura tenacitatis et avaritiae vitio maculantur et pecuniae quaestui et lucris attentae sunt vigilique aure sollicitae. *De Amore* p. 196; Parry, p. 200. Ad haec mulier omnis

non solum naturaliter reperitur avara, sed etiam invida et aliarum maledica, rapax, ventris obsequio dedita, inconstans, in sermone multiplex, inobediens et contra interdicta renitens, superbiae vitio maculata et inanis gloriae cupida, mendax, ebriosa, verlingosa, nil secretum servans, nimis luxuriosa, ad omne malum prona et hominem cordis affectione non amans. *De Amore,* p. 197; Parry, p. 201.

[50]Quia corporis pudicitia et abstinentia carnis res est, quam apud Deum et homines expedit cunctis habere et eam modis omnibus conservare, quin ea neglecta nullum in homine bonum posset esse perfectum plene. *De Amore,* p. 193; Parry, p. 198.

[51]Parry, p. 187. Nullus enim posset per aliqua benefacta Deo placere, quousque voluerit amoris inservire ministeriis. *De Amore,* p. 181.

[52]Haec igitur nostra subtiliter et fideliter examinata doctrina, quam tibi praesenti libello mandamus insertam, tibi duplicem sententiam propinabit. *De Amore,* p. 208; Parry, pp. 210-211.

[53]Odit namque Deus et utroque iussit testamento puniri, quos extra nuptiales actus agnoscit Veneris operibus

obligari vel quocunque voluptatis genere detineri. *De Amore,* pp. 181-182; Parry, p. 187.

[54]Nam ex amore proximus laeditur, quem ex mandato divino quisque tanquam se ipsum iubetur diligere. *De Amore,* 182; Parry, p. 188.

[55]Alia quoque ratio crimen nobis contradicit amoris. Nam, quum omnia crimina ipsam animam tantum de sui soleant inquinare natura, istud crimen solum animam simul cum corpore foedat, ergo super omnibus est criminibus evitandum, unde non immerito evidenter divina clamat auctoritas, crimen nullum esse gravius fornicatione repertum. *De Amore,* p. 184; Parry, p. 189.

[56]O, quam mirabile debet cunctis illud sapere bonum, quod viventibus poenam sine intermissione promittit et morientibus cruciatus minatur aeternos, illamque amantibus universis spondet hereditatem, quam in tenebris exterioribus sitam evangelica Scriptura demonstrat, ubi scilicet fletus et stridor dentium erit. *De Amore,* p. 186; Parry, pp. 191-192.

[57]Praeterea ipsum Deum sine omni dubitatione castitatis et pudicitiae caput esse scimus atque principium;

diabolum vero amoris et luxuriae auctorem esse, scriptura referente cognovimus. *De Amore,* p. 189; Parry, pp. 194-195.

[58]Amor enim inique matrimonia frangit et cogit sine causa ab uxore avertere virum. *De Amore,* p. 191; Parry, p. 196.

[59]Quos Deus lege data firmiter non posse statuit ab homine separari. Ait enim Scriptura: "Quos Deus coniunxit, homo non separet." Immo iam plures novimus coamantium, eos amore cogente in uxoris interitum cogitare ac eas crudelissima trucidatione necare, quod cunctis constat scelus esse nefandum. In hoc enim saeculo nihil debet aliquis homo tanta affectione diligere quanta uxorem, quae legitimo est sibi iure coniuncta. Nam cum viro carnem unam Deus indicavit uxorem et aliis cunctis relictis uxori iussit adhaerere maritum. Ait enim: "Propter hoc relinquet homo patrem et matrem et adhaerebit uxori suae, et erunt duo in carne una [persona]." *De Amore, ibid.;* Parry, *ibid.*

[60]Librum etiam "De Amore," sive, "De Deo amoris," qui sic incipit: Cogit me multum, etc., et sic terminatur: Cave, igitur, Galtere, amoris exercere mandata,

etc. *Chartularium Universitatis Parisiensis* I, ed. Denifle et Chatelain (Paris, 1889), p. 543; Pierre Mandonnet, *Siger de Brabant et l'Averroïsme latin au XIIIᵐᵉ siècle* II (2nd ed., Louvain, 1908), p. 176.

[61]Magnarum et gravium personarum crebra zeloque fidei accensa insinuavit relatio, quod nonnulli Parisius studentes in artibus propriae facultatis limites excedentes quosdam manifestos et execrabiles errores, immo potius vanitates et insanias falsas in rotulo seu cedulis, presentibus hiis annexo seu annexis contentos quasi dubitabiles in scolis tractare et disputare presumunt. *Chartularium,* p. 543; Mandonnet, p. 175.

[62]Dicunt enim ea esse vera secundum philosophiam, sed non secundum fidem catholicam, quasi sint due contrarie veritates, et quasi contra veritatem sacrae scripturae sit veritas in dictis gentilium dampnatorum. *Chartularium,* p. 543; Mandonnet, p. 175.

[63]Cf. Pierre Mandonnet, *Siger de Brabant* I, p. 160.

[64]Cf. Georges de Lagarde, *La Naissance de l'esprit laïque au déclin du moyen âge* II, (Paris, 1934), pp. 84-86.

81

[65]Cf. Fernand van Steenberghen, *Siger de Brabant* **II**, (Louvain, 1942), pp. 378-389.

[66]Etienne Gilson, *La Philosophie au moyen âge* (2nd ed., Paris, 1944), p. 589.

[67]"La Doctrine de la double vérité" in Etienne Gilson, *Etudes de philosophie mediévale* (Strasbourg, 1921), pp. 51-69, and F. Sassen, "Siger de Brabant et la doctrine de la double vérité," *Revue néo-scholastique de philosophie* (1931), pp. 170-179.

[68]Quod sapientes mundi sunt philosophi tantum. *Chartularium,* No. 154, p. 552; Mandonnet, No. 2, p. 176.

[69]Quod nichil est credendum, nisi per se notum, vel ex per se notis possit declarari. *Chartularium,* No. 37, p. 545; Mandonnet, No. 4, p. 177.

[70]Quod lex christiana impedit addiscere. *Chartularium,* No. 175, p. 553; Mandonnet, No. 180, p. 189.

[71]Quod sermones theologi fundati sunt in fabulis. *Chartularium,* No. 152, p. 552; Mandonnet, No. 183, p. 189.

[72]Etienne Gilson, *art. cit.*, p. 68.

[73]Quaerimus enim hic solum intentionem philosophorum et praecipue Aristotelis, etsi forte Philosophus
senserit aliter quam veritas se habeat et per revela-
tionem aliqua de anima tradita sint, quae per rationes
naturales concludi non possunt. *Quaestiones de anima
intellectiva,* ed. Pierre Mandonnet, *Siger de Brabant*
II, pp. 153-154.

[74]Circa septimum prius propositionum, videlicet utrum
anima intellectiva multiplicetur multiplicatione corporum humanorum, diligenter considerandum est,
quantum pertinet ad philosophum, et ut ratione humana et experientia comprehendi potest, quaerendo
intentionem philosophorum, in hoc magis quam veritatem, cum philosophice procedamus. Certum est
enim secundum veritatem quae mentiri non potest,
quod animae intellectivae multiplicantur multiplicatione corporum humanorum. Tamen aliqui philosophi
contrarium senserunt. *Ibid.,* p. 164.

[75]Hoc dicimus sensisse Philosophum de unione animae
intellectivae ad corpus; sententiam tamen sanctae
fidei catholicae, si contraria huic sit sententiae Philosophi, praeferre volentes, sicut et in aliis qui-

buscumque. *Ibid.,* pp. 156-157. Et iterum, Philosophus vult intellectum esse in potentia ad species in-
telligibiles, et receptivum specierum, et denudatum a
speciebus, quod si sit unus, erit semper plenus speciebus et destruetur intellectus agens. Et ideo dico
propter difficultatem praemissorum et quorumdam
aliorum, quod mihi dubium fuit a longo tempore,
quid via rationis naturalis in praedicto problemate
sit tenendum, et quid senserit Philosophus de dicta
quaestione; et in tali dubio fidei adhaerendum est,
quae omnem rationem humanam superat. *Ibid.,* p.
169.

[76]Cf. Etienne Gilson, *Reason and Revelation in the
Middle Ages* (New York, 1938), pp. 58-60, and *La
Philosophie au moyen âge,* pp. 561-563.

[77]Non expedit, ergo, venerande amice, tuos in amore
consumere dies, quem tot superius improbatum ra-
tionibus constat. Nam, si te facit regis gratia carere
coelestis et omni te penitus vero privat amico et huius
saeculi cunctos subducit honores, omnisque famae
laudabilis per eundem supprimitur aura, ac sui vora-
citate divitias devorat universas, et ex eo, sicut superius narratur, mala cuncta sequuntur, cur stulte,
quaeris amare, vel quod inde posses acquirere bonum,

quod tibi valeret tot incommoda compensare? . . . .
Si cuncta igitur, quae in amore versantur, vigili cura-
veris mente perquirere, clara poteris veritate cognoscere, quam inevitabili quisque ratione tenetur
amorem totis viribus evitare et eius penitus calcare
mandata. *De Amore,* pp. 207-208; Parry, p. 210.

> [78]*Essa è la luce eterna di Sigieri,*
> *Che, leggendo nel vico degli strami,*
> *Sillogizzò invidiosi veri.*

Paradiso X, 136-138.

[79]Cf. Etienne Gilson, *Dante et la philosophie* (Paris,
1939), pp. 269-273.

[80]Dante's separation of the political and the spiritual,
of the philosophical and the theological, is certainly
not that advocated and taught by Averroes himself
in the *Agreement of Religion and Philosophy.* Nor
is there any indication that Dante ever taught any
of the theses defined as averroistic or ever accepted as
rationally necessary a single philosophical conclusion
at variance with Christian dogma and revelation. The
only tie that the *De Monarchia* has with Latin Averroism is the separation of the two orders. His purpose in

accepting such a teaching and placing it in the service of politics was not to arouse conflicts between the two orders, of subjugating the theological and spiritual to the rule and use of the philosophical and the natural, but to unite and coordinate them. Cf. Etienne Gilson, *Dante et la philosophie,* pp. 210-216; *La Philosophie au moyen âge,* p. 578. In fact, Gilson is inclined to think that the *De Monarchia* is not a particular case of Latin Averroism but rather an attempt on the part of Dante to establish his doctrine of political separation on the moral philosophy of Aristotle's *Nicomachean Ethics* and on the commentary of St. Thomas upon it. Cf. Gilson, *Dante et la philosophie,* pp. 215-222.

[81]That separation emerges most clearly and succinctly in the concluding chapter of the Third Book: *De Monarchia* III, 16, ed. Edward Moore (Oxford, 1916), pp. 375-376.

[82]Léon Gautier, *La Théorie d'Ibn Roschd sur les rapports de la religion et de la philosophie* (Paris, 1909), pp. 174-175.

[83]Cf. Léon Gautier, *op. cit.,* pp. 19-30; *Introduction à*

l'étude de la philosophie musulmane (Paris, 1923),
pp. 68-120; Louis Gardet, "Raison et foi en Islam,"
Revue Thomiste XLIII (1937), pp. 439-478; XLIV
(1938), pp. 145-167; 342-378.

[84]Cf. Louis Gardet, "Quelques aspects de la pensée
avicennienne dans ses rapports avec l'orthodoxie musulmane," *Revue Thomiste* XLV (1939), pp. 537-
575; 693-742, especially p. 741.

[85]With the theory of prophecy was bound up the question of divine truth, for the two are identified. Revelation, dogma, religious law, moral teaching, social and
political precepts derive from it. Al-Farabi and Avicenna taught that there is nothing supernatural as
such in prophecy. It does not go beyond the faculties
or powers of the human intellect, but is simply the
highest capacity of the human intellect put into act
by an emanation of the Agent Intelligence. Thus,
the content of faith is made accessible to reason and
there is no order of knowledge beyond the rational.
Only those, however, who are gifted by God with
certain natural qualities which make them the most
perfect representatives of the human race are apt for
such illumination. Cf. Léon Gautier, *La Théorie de*

Ibn Roschd, pp. 167-170 and Louis Gardet, "Quelques aspects de la pensée avicennienne," pp. 708-720, especially p. 716.

86Cf. Louis Gardet, "Raison et foi en Islam," *Revue Thomiste* XLIV (1938), p. 146 ff.; A. R. Nicholson "Origin and Development of Sufism," *Journal of the Royal Asiatic Society* (1906), pp. 306-348; Louis Massignon, *The Encyclopedia of Islam,* IV² (London, 1929), *art.* Tasawwuf.

87Cf. Louis Gardet, "Raison et foi en Islam," *Revue Thomiste* XLIV (1938), pp. 166-168; Léon Gautier, *op. cit.,* p. 173.

88*Les Trois dernières sections de l'ouvrage al-Ishârât wa-t-Tanbîhât* (Indications et Annotations VIIIᵉ section, *Traités mystiques d'Aboû Alî al-Hosain b. Abdallâh b. Sînâ ou d'Avicenne,* ed. M. A. F. Mehrens (Leyde, 1891), p. 5.

89Nous t'avons régalé, mon frère, de la crème de la vérité et des mets exquis de la sagesse; garde cette dissertation à l'abri de toute profanation des ignorants, privés de l'illumination d'en haut et de la pratique, dont les penchants sont du côté du vulgaire, et qui rejettent ces vérités tout comme nos soi-disants philosophes renommés, eux et leurs adhérents, par leur incrédulité; mais si tu rencontres un homme sûr et à l'abri de toute mauvaise influence, qui, cherchant Dieu, est favorisé de la lumière, de la grâce et de la vérité, satisfais ses demandes peu à peu et partiellement, et fais lui espérer la continuation de ton intimité future, si tu observes chez lui de bonnes suites de ta confiance passée, mais oblige-le pourtant par des serments solennels d'observer la même méthode que toi-même et de se conformer à ton exemple; au contraire, si tu répands cette doctrine indiscrètement et en abuses, sache que le Dieu très haut sera juge entre toi et moi. *Ibid.*, p. 21.

[90]Cf. W. Heyd, *Histoire du commerce du Levant au moyen âge* (Leipzig, 1923), pp. 181-188; Miguel Asín Palacios, *La Escatología musulmana en la Divina Comedia* (Madrid, 1919), pp. 299-308; Louis Bréhier, *L'Eglise et l'orient au moyen âge* (Paris, 1907), pp. 89-100; A. R. Nykl, *The Dove's Neck-Ring* (Paris, 1931), pp. xl-lxxvi.

[91]Cf. A. J. Denomy, *"Fin' Amors:* The Pure Love of the Troubadours, its Amorality, and Possible Source," *Mediaeval Studies* VII (1945), pp. 189-205.

[92]Lawrence Ecker, *Arabischer, provenzalischer und deutscher Minnesang* (Diss. Bonn, 1934).

[93]A. R. Nykl, *The Dove's Neck-Ring,* pp. xc-ci; *Hispano-Arabic Poetry and its Relations with the Old Provençal Troubadours* (Baltimore, 1946), pp. 382-393; Ramón Menéndez Pidal, "Poesía árabe y Poesía europea," *Bulletin Hispanique* XL (1938), pp. 337-391.

[94]Andreas tells us why he wrote the *De Reprobatione:* Taliter igitur praesentem lege libellum, non quasi per ipsum quaerens amantium tibi assumere vitam, sed ut eius doctrina refectus et mulierum edoctus ad amandum animos provocare a tali provocatione abstinendo praemium consequaris aeternum et maiori ex hoc apud Deum merearis munere gloriari. *De Amore,* p. 181; Parry, p. 187. Quem tractatum nostrum si attenta volueris investigatione disquirere ac mentis intellectu percipere et eiusdem doctrinam operis executione compere, ratione manifesta cognosces, neminem in amoris voluptatibus debere male suos expendere dies, ac inde rex coelestis in cunctis tibi propitius permanebit et in hoc saeculo prosperos mereberis habere successus et universa laudabilia et honesta desideria cordis implere, ac in futuro gloriam

et vitam possidebis aeternam. *De Amore,* p. 208; Parry, p. 211.

[95]Cf., for example, J. J. Parry, *op. cit.,* p. 19.

[96]Cf. E. K. Rand, *Ovid and his Influence* (Boston, 1925), pp. 48-54; Hermann Fränkel, *Ovid: a Poet between Two Worlds* (Berkeley, California, 1945), pp. 68-70.

[97]Therefore, it is manifestly unfair to Andreas to evaluate his worth as a cleric and to judge of his sincerity as a churchman on the basis of the *De Amore* proper. There he is writing neither as a cleric nor as a churchman, but as a rational and natural man to whom the office of cleric is something extrinsic and accidental conferred upon him, concerning a subject that is wholly natural. Spiritual affairs are not his first consideration; in fact, they are of no consideration whatsoever. In the *De Reprobatione,* he is on a totally different level—that of the spiritual and theological, in contrast to the natural and philosophical of the *De Amore.* If Andreas must be judged as a cleric and churchman, then the evaluation must be made from the basis of the *De Reprobatione* rather than that of the *De Amore.*

[98]Cf. Tom Peete Cross and William Albert Nitze, *Lancelot and Guinevere, a Study on the Origins of Courtly Love* (Chicago, 1930), pp. 67-68.

[99]ll. 1835-1848.

[100]Karl Young, "Chaucer's Renunciation of Love in *Troilus and Cressida*," *Modern Language Notes* XL (1925), pp. 270 ff.